Rachel Carson
Saving the Environment

Rory Queenston

INFOMAX
COMMON CORE
READERS

Rosen
Classroom™

New York

Published in 2014 by The Rosen Publishing Group, Inc.
29 East 21st Street, New York, NY 10010

Book Design: Jon D'Rozario

Photo Credits: Cover (Rachel Carson) Stock Montage/Archive Photos/Getty Images; cover (background) Triff/
Shutterstock.com; pp. 3, 4, 6, 8, 10, 12, 14, 16, 18, 20, 22, 23, 24 (background) kanate/Shutterstock.com; pp. 5, 9, 17, 19
Alfred Eisenstaedt/Time & Life Pictures/Getty Images; p. 7 http://commons.wikimedia.org/wiki/File:Gilman_Hall,_Johns_
Hopkins_University,_Baltimore,_MD.jpg; pp. 11, 13 Associated Press/apimages; p. 15 B Brown/Shutterstock.com;
p. 21 Morgan Lane Photography/Shutterstock.com; p. 22 Laias/Shutterstock.com.

ISBN: 978-1-4777-2479-8
6-pack ISBN: 978-1-4777-2481-1

Manufactured in the United States of America

CPSIA Compliance Information: Batch #CS13RC: For further information contact Rosen Publishing, New York, New York at 1-800-237-9932.

EB Car

Rachel Carson
Saving the Environment

Rory Queenston

Contents

An Important Ecologist

Rachel Carson was one of the most important ecologists to ever live. An ecologist is a person who studies the **relationship** between living things and their **environment**. Rachel was a scientist and writer whose books showed people the importance of taking care of the environment.

Rachel was born on May 27, 1907, in Springdale, Pennsylvania. She learned about nature by playing outside in the forests near her family's farm. Rachel loved learning about the different plants and animals around her.

Rachel's writings explained that humans were a part of the natural world rather than separate from it.

5

At School

Rachel loved nature, and she loved writing. She was a good writer from an early age. When she was 10 years old, some of her writing was **published** in a children's magazine!

Rachel went to the Pennsylvania **College** for Women. She studied English because she loved to write. However, she changed her mind and began studying science before finishing college in 1929. She then studied science at a school called Johns Hopkins University.

Rachel finished studying at Johns Hopkins University in 1932. She studied zoology, or the science of animals.

Working for the Government

After Rachel finished studying at Johns Hopkins University, she began working for the U.S. government. Her job was to write radio programs about fish and other sea creatures. Rachel also wrote about **protecting** nature in magazines and newspapers.

In 1936, Rachel began working as a scientist and editor for the government. She held this job for 15 years. Rachel eventually became editor in chief of all writings published by the U.S. Fish and Wildlife Service.

Rachel worked for the government until 1952. She left to spend more time writing books about nature.

Books About Ecology

Rachel's first book was published in 1941. It was called *Under the Sea-Wind* and was about the birds and sea creatures that lived near the ocean in the eastern United States. Rachel wrote in a way that made people care about the environment.

In 1951, Rachel's second book, *The Sea Around Us*, was published. This book told readers about the history of the ocean. *The Sea Around Us* was a very popular book. It sold enough copies to be called a best seller!

Rachel's books helped people learn about ecology and understand the natural world.

The Sea Around Us also became popular in other countries. It was published in 32 different languages! Rachel won many **awards** for this book, including the National Book Award.

Rachel wrote a third book about the ocean, which was published in 1955. *The Edge of the Sea* was another book that opened readers' eyes to the importance of respecting and protecting the environment. Rachel made Americans care about ecology with her beautiful words and important facts.

Rachel wrote a lot about the ocean, but she knew that all parts of the environment needed to be protected to keep Earth healthy.

Rachel Carson

▼

The Pesticide Problem

After she wrote *The Edge of the Sea*, Rachel began planning a book about pesticides, which are **chemicals** sprayed on plants to kill harmful bugs. She thought pesticides would kill more than just bugs. They could destroy an entire ecosystem, or community of living things.

Rachel believed the most harmful pesticide was one called DDT. She wanted to tell people about its dangers before it was too late.

Rachel knew it was important to warn people about the dangers of using harmful pesticides such as DDT.

15

Rachel worked hard to gather facts about pesticides for her book, which was called *Silent Spring*. The title came from Rachel's fear that pesticides would someday cause birds and other animals to die, making the environment silent. *Silent Spring* was published in 1962 and became Rachel's most popular book.

Silent Spring made readers see the connections between all living things in an ecosystem. Rachel wrote that it was our job as humans to protect nature, but pesticides were harming nature instead.

Silent Spring is still Rachel's most famous book. It changed the way many people looked at their role in the environment.

After *Silent Spring* was published, the U.S. government studied pesticides to see if Rachel was right about their dangers. Rachel even spoke to Congress about the harmful effects of DDT. The government eventually found that Rachel was right, and DDT was banned in the United States.

Rachel didn't live long after *Silent Spring* was published. She died on April 14, 1964, after many years of being sick. Rachel lives on in her books and other writings about nature.

We remember Rachel Carson as a woman who changed the way we look at nature.

Remembering Rachel

Rachel Carson is often thought of as the creator of the modern environmentalist movement. Her books, especially *Silent Spring*, made Americans realize the importance of caring for Earth and understanding the role of every living thing in an ecosystem.

Rachel's work led to the creation of a special department in the U.S. government for the care and protection of the environment. The Environmental Protection Agency was formed in 1970 and is still active today.

Rachel believed that every living thing had a part to play in its environment. How can you keep the environment healthy?

An Ecologist's Life

Rachel is born on May 27 in Springdale, Pennsylvania.

1907

1929 Rachel finishes studying at the Pennsylvania College for Women.

Rachel finishes studying at Johns Hopkins University.

1932

1941 *Under the Sea-Wind* is published.

The Sea Around Us is published.

1951

1955 *The Edge of the Sea* is published.

Silent Spring is published.

1962

1964 Rachel dies on April 14.

Glossary

award (uh-WOHRD) A prize given for doing something well.

chemical (KEH-mih-kuhl) Matter that can be mixed with other matter to cause changes.

college (KAH-lihj) A school that young adults go to after they finish high school.

environment (ihn-VY-ruhn-muhnt) The natural world around us.

protect (pruh-TEHKT) To keep safe.

publish (PUH-blish) To print a written work and present it to the public.

relationship (ree-LAY-shun-ship) A connection between two or more things.

Index